COUNTRIES IN THE NEWS

JAPAN

Kieran Walsh

Vero Beach, Florida 32964

www.rourkepublishing.com

The country's flag is correct at the time of going to press.

PHOTO CREDITS: ©Yoshikazu Tsuno/AFP/Getty Images Cover;
©Fabel Nard pg 4; ©Woorija pg 16; ©Steve Matthews pg 12; All other images
© Peter Langer Associated Media Group

Title page: *Cherry blossoms adorn a temple in Nikko.*

Editor: Frank Sloan

Cover and interior design by Nicola Stratford

Library of Congress Cataloging-in-Publication Data

Walsh, Kieran.
Japan / Kieran Walsh.
p. cm. -- (Countries in the news)
Includes bibliographical references and index.
ISBN 1-59515-289-X (hardcover)
1. Japan--Social life and customs--1945---Juvenile literature. I. Title. II. Series: Walsh, Kieran. Countries in the news ; v 11.
DS822.5.W33 2004

2004009688.

Printed in the USA

CG/CG

TABLE OF CONTENTS

WELCOME TO JAPAN

Japan is a nation made up of several thousand islands. The four main islands are Honshu, Hokkaido, Kyushu, and Shikoku. Tokyo, Japan's capital and largest city, is on Honshu, the biggest island.

Tokyo bustles with crowds, just like many of the world's cities.

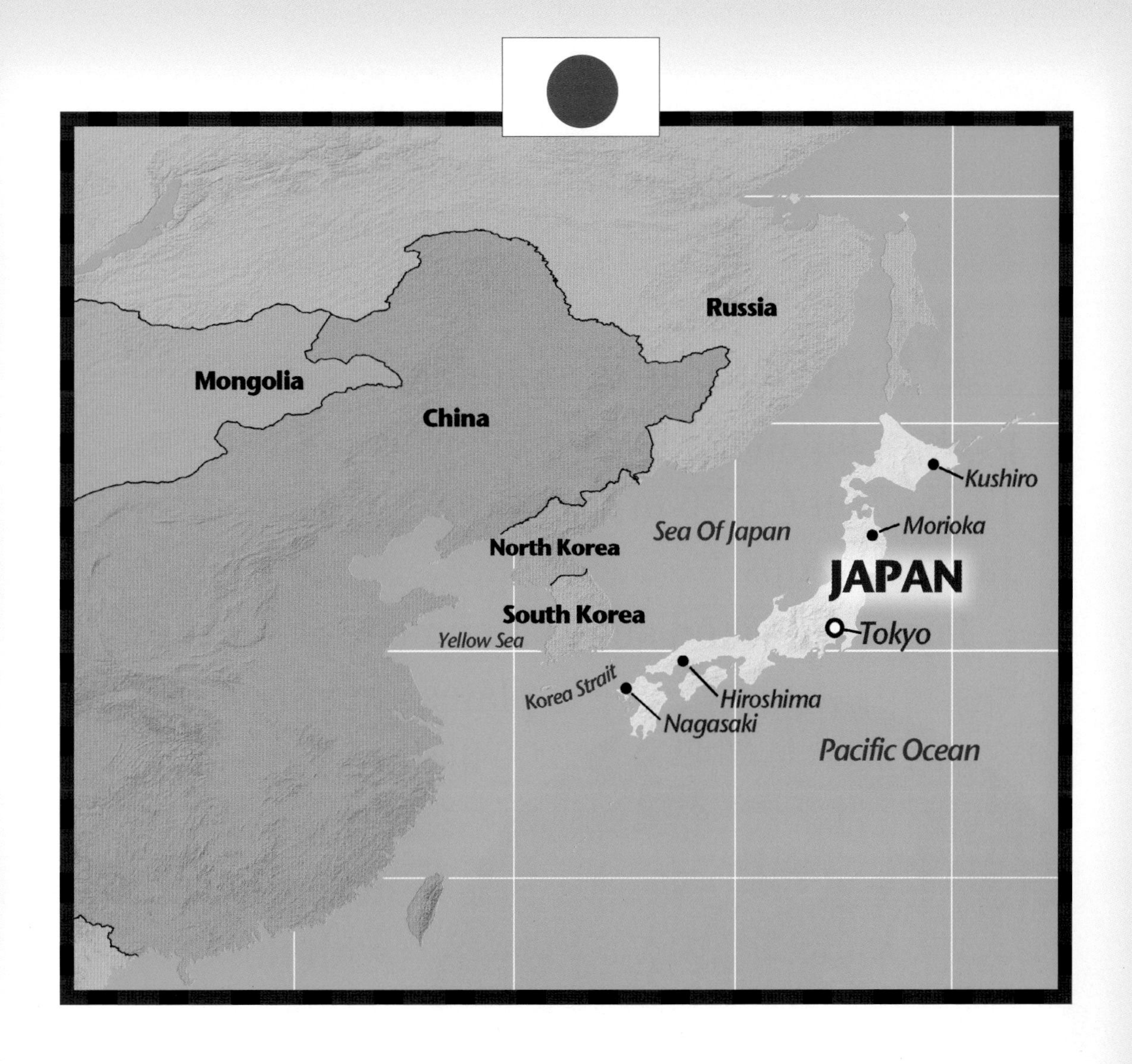

Japan is located in the Pacific Ocean not far from Korea, Russia, and China. Including its islands, Japan is about the same size as the state of Montana. In 2003, the population of Japan was more than 127 million.

Most Japanese live on Honshu.

Much of Japan is mountainous. The largest peak in Japan is Mount Fuji, which reaches up 12,388 feet (3,776 m). Mount Fuji is part of the Japanese Alps.

Japan is located above a number of **oceanic** plates, making it a high-risk area for earthquakes. In order to deal with this threat, the Japanese are always prepared.

A Tokyo store owner shows off his products for sale.

Mount Fuji towers above the landscape.

Most homes have an emergency kit with water, flashlight, and bandages. Japanese children are taught from an early age to remain indoors during an earthquake and stay calm.

THE PEOPLE

Because there are many Japanese and most live in cities like Tokyo, living space is very expensive. Finding an apartment can be difficult. In the countryside, though, most people still live in wood houses with walls made from paper.

These Japanese teenagers are like young people the world over.

A mother and her child in Hiroshima

The Japanese have a strong focus on the family unit. Though many women do work, they are usually expected to stay home and raise children. Most Japanese women are married by the age of 25.

The two major religions of Japan are Shintoism and Buddhism. Shintoism involves the worship of **supernatural** beings called *kami*. Followers of this religion pray in **shrines** marked by giant, red gates called *torii*. Buddhism, meanwhile, is a religion that came from India through China.

Though many Japanese wear clothing similar to what we wear in the United States, a more **traditional** garment, the kimono, is also popular. A kimono is a long, colorful dress worn by Japanese women.

The bronze statue of the Great Buddha in Nara

At a show in Kyoto, women are dressed in kimonos.

Practicing Buddhists often work toward a state of deep relaxation called **meditation**.

LIFE IN JAPAN

Japan is one of the most **technologically** advanced countries in the world. Cellular phones, personal computers, and DVD players are as common as in the United States.

A busy intersection in Tokyo

With such a large population, public transportation is very important.

The Japanese "bullet train" is one of the fastest in the world. It can travel at speeds of more than 150 miles (241 km) per hour.

A bullet train stops at a station.

SCHOOL AND SPORTS

The Japanese take education very seriously. Most Japanese children attend school every day except Sunday. Meanwhile, their summer vacations last a little more than one month. All of this study is preparation for attending one of Japan's 500 universities. For the Japanese, the school students go to is more important than the grades they receive. Many sports popular in Japan, like Karate and Judo, have also gained a following in the United States.

A family leaves paper cranes at the peace memorial in Hiroshima.

Japanese schoolchildren

Likewise, American baseball is a Japanese favorite. Sumo, a kind of wrestling match between extremely heavy men, is also popular.

The **literacy** rate in Japan is 99 percent.

FOOD AND HOLIDAYS

The most famous of all Japanese foods is often referred to as *sushi*. Sushi is usually a combination of raw fish and sticky rice. Sometimes these ingredients are bundled into a roll. For seasoning, people use soy sauce and wasabi—a very hot Japanese horseradish. A favorite drink with a sushi meal is often green tea.

Rolled sushi, a great favorite among the Japanese

An outdoor food vendor in Kyoto

The most important holiday in Japan is Shogatsu, or New Year's Day. Shogatsu takes place from January 1 to January 3.

The Japanese believe that the first day of a new year sets the tone for the rest of that year. On January 1, everyone in Japan makes an effort to be happy and polite.

A loving grandmother and her grandson

The temple at Nara, which was built in A.D. 752.

THE FUTURE

Although Japan is not as prosperous as it was during the 1980s, efforts are being made to strengthen the economy. There is no doubt that the Japanese **emphasis** on education and family will ensure the survival and growth of the country.

Perhaps that continual hope for the future is why the symbol of the Japanese flag is a rising sun.

FAST FACTS

Area: 145,882 square miles (377,805 sq km)

Borders: Japan is surrounded by water. The Sea of Japan separates it from the eastern coast of Asia. To the east of Japan is the Pacific Ocean.

Population: 127,214,499 **Monetary Unit:** Yen

Largest Cities: Tokyo, Yokohama, Osaka, Nagoya, Kobe

Government: Constitutional monarchy

Religion: Shintoist, Buddhist, Christian

Crops: Rice, sugar beets, vegetables, fruit

Natural Resources: Fish, minerals

Major Industries: Motor vehicles, electronics, machine tools, steel, chemicals, textiles

WORLD WAR II

For many years now, Japan and the United States have been close **allies**. There was a time, though, when the two countries were bitter enemies.

During World War II (1939-1945), Japan was one of three Axis powers, including Germany and Italy. It was the Japanese attack on Pearl Harbor on December 7, 1941, that pushed the United States into the war.

Japan was eventually defeated after **atomic** bombs were dropped on the cities of Hiroshima and Nagasaki. Japan formally surrendered on September 2, 1945.

The Toshogu shrine is a five-story-high pagoda.

GLOSSARY

allies (AL EYEZ) — friends

atomic (uh TOM ik) — using the power of the atom

emphasis (EM fuh sis) — a focus on

literacy (LIT eh ruh see) — the ability to read and write

meditation (MED uh TAY shun) — a concentrated form of deep relaxation

oceanic (OH shee AN ik) — relating to the ocean

shrines (SHRYNES) — sacred places of religious worship

supernatural (SOO pur NATCH e ruhl) — having to do with the spiritual; beyond the normal world

technologically (TEK nuh laj ih kul ee) — relating to the use of science and machines to make life easier

traditional (truh DISH uh nul) — common; typical

FURTHER READING

Find out more about Japan with these helpful books:

- Behnke, Alison. *Visual Geography: Japan in Pictures*. Lerner Publications, 2003.
- Bramwell, Martyn. *The World in Maps: Australia, The Pacific, and Antarctica*. Lerner Publications, 2000.
- Costain, Meredith, and Paul Collins. *Welcome to Japan*. Chelsea House, 2001.
- Greene, Meg. *Japan: A Primary Source Cultural Guide*. Rosen Publication Group, 2004.
- Kalman, Bobbie. *Japan: The Land.* Crabtree Publications, 2000.
- Lansford, Lewis, and Chris Schwarz. *The Changing Face of Japan*. Raintree/Steck Vaughn, 2002.
- Park, Ted. *Taking Your Camera to Japan*. Steadwell Books, 2000.

WEBSITE TO VISIT

- gojapan.about.com/index.htm?terms=japan
  About.com – Japan for Visitors

INDEX

About the Author

Kieran Walsh is a writer of children's nonfiction books, primarily on historical and social studies topics. Walsh has been involved in the children's book field as editor, proofreader, and illustrator as well as author.